Eat th Rainbow

Hawys Morgan

Illustrated by Feronia Parker-Thomas

Schofield & Sims

Maisie didn't like fruit. She and Dad had lots of discussions about it.

He thought she should eat five portions of fruit and vegetables every day. She disagreed.

I just don't like fruit!

That summer, Maisie flew to Jamaica to visit Grandma for the first time.

They travelled from the bus station past sugar
plantations and mansions.

On the bus, Dad described the pretty location of Grandma's house in the hills.

When they arrived, Maisie explored the garden. It was even more beautiful than Dad's description!

Grandma sent Maisie on a special mission to find ripe mangoes, passion fruit and sugar apples.

Maisie jumped into action. She raced around the garden, looking for the fruit.

She only came inside when there was a torrential rain shower.

Grandma cut open a sugar apple, but Maisie wouldn't try it.

I just don't like fruit!

Grandma went into the kitchen and returned with a smoothie for Maisie.

Maisie wiped the sugary juice from her lips with a tissue.

That was yummy!

"Did I mention that the smoothie was made from the fruit you picked?" asked Grandma.

Maisie looked at Grandma with a shocked expression.

Are you sure?

How had Grandma turned fruit into something so tasty?

Maisie decided to try the sugar apple. It was sweet and creamy.

She bit into passion fruit seeds. They were a crunchy, sweet explosion!

Maisie asked Grandma's permission to pick more
fruit from the garden.

"You can pick as much fruit as you like, on condition that you eat it!" smiled Grandma.

Maisie picked watermelon, mangoes, pineapple, starfruit and grapes.

She carefully prepared and arranged the fruit in different sections.

I hope Grandma will like it!

They ate avocadoes and tomatoes for lunch.
It was all fresh. Nothing was artificial.

Then Maisie fetched the special fruit salad she had made for Grandma.